Songs of Discovery for Music Therapy

SONGS OF DISCOVERY FOR MUSIC THERAPY

A Practical Resource for Therapists and Educators

The Center for Discovery®

Edited by
Conio Loretto and Amanda Ruddy Belcastro

Jessica Kingsley Publishers
London and Philadelphia

First published in Great Britain in 2023 by Jessica Kingsley Publishers
An imprint of John Murray Press

1

A CIP catalogue record for this title is available from the
British Library and the Library of Congress

ISBN 978 1 83997 753 4
eISBN 978 1 83997 754 1

Printed and bound in the United States by Integrated Books International

Jessica Kingsley Publishers' policy is to use papers that are natural, renewable and recyclable
products and made from wood grown in sustainable forests. The logging and manufacturing
processes are expected to conform to the environmental regulations of the country of origin.

Jessica Kingsley Publishers
Carmelite House
50 Victoria Embankment
London EC4Y 0DZ

www.jkp.com

John Murray Press
Part of Hodder & Stoughton Limited
An Hachette UK Company

This collection is dedicated to the remarkable children and adults of The Center for Discovery.

Contents

Foreword

At The Center for Discovery (TCFD), we pursue deep, meaningful human expression every day. We feel that no one works harder at helping individuals with complex conditions find and foster their expression than our music therapy team.

The words "no" and "limitation" are simply not in our music therapists' vocabulary. They uncover ways for children and adults who have a hard time with things like fine motor skills to experience rhythm. They find ways to help them discover their voices – even though some of the individuals in our care cannot speak. They understand that music is the universal language that communicates in places deep within each of us. They understand that there's community in those places. And they know that building this community leads to even more self-expression.

TCFD's team of renowned music therapists consider every note and every word. It is experienced, intentional work. In the pages ahead, you will find a selection of songs that will be a great resource for clinicians, educators, and parents alike. You may even discover information about why music is so important to every human being – and how music can connect us all.

Allow yourself the time to take in this rich knowledge as you journey into the music. We know it will be a high note of your work in music rooms, classrooms, and studios across the globe.

Patrick H. Dollard, CEO, The Center for Discovery

Acknowledgements

Patrick Dollard

Terry Hamlin

Richard Humleker

Michael Rosen

Helena le Roux Ohm

Jim Cashen

Kerri Muzuruk

Courtney Scott

Dean McManus

Jessica Calabrese

Julie Johnson Abrams

Dan Wenger

Betsey King

Meghan Smith

Cliff Schlosser Loretto

Stephen Belcastro

Music transcription services provided by Collin DeJoseph (www.collindejoseph. com).

Contributing Composers

Conio Loretto, MS, LCAT, MT-BC, Editor
Senior Director of Music Therapy, The Center for Discovery
Adjunct professor, State University of New York at New Paltz

Amanda Ruddy Belcastro, MT-BC, Editor
Senior music therapist, The Center for Discovery

Beth Deyermond, MA, MT-BC
Director of Music Therapy, The Center for Discovery
Adjunct professor, State University of New York at New Paltz

Rebecca Erson, MS, MT-BC
Music therapist, The Center for Discovery

Kenny Farinelli, MT-BC
Music therapist, The Center for Discovery

Stacey Hensel, MA, LCAT, MT-BC, NRMT
Music therapy department supervisor, The Rebecca School

Miyoung Lee, MS, MT-BC
Music therapist
Founder, My Cozy Piano

Lee Anne Miller
Music therapist, private practice

Nicholas Sherman, MT-BC
Music therapist, The Center for Discovery

About The Center For Discovery

The Center for Discovery (TCFD) is a leading provider of healthcare and education services for more than 1200 children and adults with complex conditions, medical frailties, and on the autism spectrum. Located 90 miles northwest of New York City, TCFD was named a Center of Excellence in 2016 and has long been a leader in developing new models of care for individuals with complex conditions. Situated on 1500 acres of land in rural Sullivan County, NY, TCFD houses school campuses, residences, medical and research facilities, organic and biodynamic farmland, and leased private businesses offering meaningful employment opportunities. Deeply focused on an individual's personal potential and possibilities rather than a disability, TCFD strives to create better care and unique and challenging opportunities for the most vulnerable populations.

The music therapy program at TCFD began in the Fall of 1997 and has since earned an international reputation within the profession. Dedicated to transforming lives through the power of music, TCFD employs a dynamic team of board-certified music therapists who work across both day and evening shifts, seven days a week. As a national roster and university-affiliated internship site approved by the American Music Therapy Association, TCFD's internship program has trained over 150 student interns from colleges and universities around the world. TCFD music therapists are dedicated to advancing knowledge within the field and regularly share their innovative work at professional conferences, within academic settings, and in publications.

www.thecenterfordiscovery.org

INTRODUCTION

Each of the songs found in this collection came to life through the engaging, creative process of music therapy at The Center for Discovery. During music therapy, individuals are engaged in the dynamic experience of creating music. They may join in the music making by playing instruments, singing, vocalizing, moving, and/or dancing. Out of the music making come opportunities for personal growth and fulfillment. The outcomes of music therapy are as varied as the individuals themselves:

- For those struggling with interacting with others, music builds connections.

- Within music therapy groups, joint music-making pursuits nurture peer relationships.

- In moments of dysregulation, the rhythmic structure of music provides a sense of order.

- For those struggling with ways to express their emotions, music provides a safe outlet.

- For those who might be feeling stuck, spontaneous music making engenders flexibility and freedom.

- For those who are physically challenged, music helps to achieve greater control in movement patterns as they entrain with a beat.

- For individuals who are having a hard time focusing, music captures and holds attention.

- As individuals become successful in the creation of their own music, confidence builds.

Songs play an important role in the therapeutic process. The predictability of a song is grounding and provides a sense of security. Songs can define a situation, signal a session is beginning or ending, or indicate that it is time to engage in a specific activity. Songs provide repetitive practice to facilitate learning without satiation. Songs outline, clarify, and reinforce the expectations of an experience. Songs help identify and express innermost thoughts and feelings. Songs provide a "home base," allowing individuals to venture away from a musical structure and have a secure place to return to.

We offer this collection of songs for use by other music therapists, music therapy students, music educators, special education teachers, and facilitators of early childhood music programs. We encourage whoever uses them to do so with great thought and intention. The songs should feel spontaneous, authentically coming to life in each moment. Use the songs freely and creatively. Perhaps they serve as the starting place and transform into a brand-new song or experience. Or maybe they inspire you to write your own song. Maybe you are drawn to a certain chord progression or lyrical phrase. Adapt the songs to meet your own unique situation. Our hope is that the songs take on a new life of their own, wherever they happen to land, and bring meaning to those who come to experience them.

Conio Loretto and Amanda Ruddy Belcastro, Editors

PDF copies of the sheets of music marked with ✻ can be downloaded from https://library.jkp.com/redeem using the code GMACSEQ

GREETING SONGS

BEAT THE DRUM TO SAY HELLO

Conio Loretto

This song was created to quickly focus the unbridled energy of a group of young children. Within the framework of the song, the children are called on to play a single beat on a hand drum. It can be effective to present the drum first in succession around the group and then in a random order to hold everyone's attention in a playful, lively manner. The single beat response provides an opportunity for the children to enjoy immediate success. Alternative lyrics can also be used to cue each group member by name (*Oh Cliff can beat the drum*).

WELCOME BACK

Stacey Hensel

This song was originally written to welcome an enthusiastic adolescent boy back to the music therapy session room. The A section has repetitive lyrics (*"welcome back"*) that are supported with an upbeat, simple blues progression. The B section includes the phrase *"we are here in music today,"* affirming the musical possibilities that lie ahead. The song can be repeated as many times as necessary to meet the unique needs and responses of the person in therapy.

WELCOME BACK TO THE MUSIC ROOM

Lee Anne Miller

This song was born of an improvised vamp created while waiting for a group of children to arrive at the music therapy session room. Each group member trickled into the room, eager for the music making to begin while excitedly vocalizing or tapping a rhythm. The first two measures of the song (the vamp) were repeated to hold each group member's musical responses before the song officially began with the lyrics *"welcome back to the music room."* The B section of the song calls on each group to offer their own musical response or greeting.

Beat the Drum to Say Hello

Conio Loretto

Playful ♩ = 118

Welcome Back

Welcome Back to the Music Room

Lee Anne Miller

Wel-come back to the mu-sic room

Wel-come back to the mu-sic room to - day

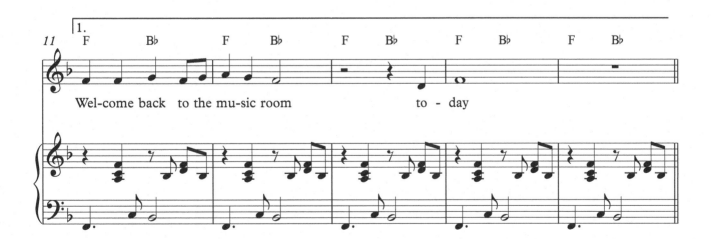

Wel-come back to the mu-sic room to - day

SONGS FOR INSTRUMENTAL PLAY

BEAT THE DRUM WHEN YOU HEAR YOUR NAME

Conio Loretto

In this song, a group of children must listen closely for the announcement of their name. Once they hear it, they are called on to reach out and play a single beat on a drum. The descending bassline in the A section provides movement towards the excitement of playing that is coming in the B section. The minor key is meant to evoke a bit of mystery. *Who is going to play? Whose name is coming next?* The B section answers definitively as each name is called on the downbeat, followed by space for the drum to sound. This song helps children recognize and respond to their name, develops turn-taking skills, and promotes emotional regulation as a sense of anticipation and controlled response is experienced.

RAISE YOUR MALLET

Amanda Ruddy Belcastro

This short piece was created for a small group of young boys who were each equipped with a mallet while a cymbal was held out for them to play. The lyrics of the song lead them to raise their mallet in the air and then crash the cymbal together in unison. The dissonance and minor key provided a playful seriousness that promoted a firm crash of the cymbal, which was an exciting prospect for the boys. The tempo for each phrase can be extended slightly with tremolos (during *"raise your mallet"*) to wait for each group member to be focused and ready. The first 12 measures can be adapted to focus on one group member at a time and then the group as a whole can come together to play in the final, slower measures of the piece.

REACH OUT

Nicholas Sherman

This song was born of a spontaneous improvisation with Jordan, a young man who relished in the opportunities presented to him in music therapy. Because of his physical limitations, reaching out to play the hanging chimes was a challenging endeavor. This piece began as an improvisation filled with rich, lush chords that Jordan responded positively to. As the music took shape, the movement of the $CMaj^7$ chord ascending to the Em^7 chord, together with the lyrics *"reach out,"* inspired Jordan to reach out and play. The improvisation grew into the song found here, which has a gentle openness where the sounds of the chimes can sparkle and shine.

REACH UP HIGH

Conio Loretto

One of Chana's clinical goals was to reach her hands high over her head as physical challenges made this a difficult task. In order for her to achieve this goal in music therapy, hanging chimes were first presented directly in front of her and then raised slowly upward so she had to reach higher and higher to produce their ringing tones. As her body entrained with the steady pulse of the music, Chana could more efficiently motor plan and accomplish this otherwise challenging task. Within the song, the energized, motivating A section is met with a slower, more fluid B section to leave room for acknowledging each time the chimes are played.

THREE FRIENDS IN THE MIDDLE

Lee Anne Miller

This song was composed for a group of young adults who thoroughly enjoyed creating music together. In it, three group members are encouraged to enter the middle of the circle to play rhythm instruments together while the other group members look on and cheer. During the A section, group members are encouraged to sing the theme, followed by the B section where the instrumentalists play. The song promotes cooperation, joint attention, and improved self-esteem.

UP AND DOWN BLUES

Amanda Ruddy Belcastro

This composition was inspired by a group of young adults who enjoyed the challenge of learning instrumental arrangements as part of their ongoing session work. The piece promotes group cohesion as well as partnership, as two players at a time are featured in each section. In the A section, the table bells in E minor pentatonic are coupled with the high and low E of the reed horns, manifesting the rise and fall of the melodic movement. The B section features the pairing of the drum and tambourine in a turn-taking fashion within the basic beat that briefly smooths the syncopation that occurs in the previous and subsequent measures.

WITH THE CRASH OF THE CYMBAL

Conio Loretto

During one of his music therapy sessions, Charlie was moving his hand up and down in a repetitive pattern. The movement suggested the possibility for musical engagement at another level for this young man who otherwise had very limited volitional movement. With adaptations to aid him in holding a mallet and with the cymbal strategically placed, Charlie experienced newfound independence. The song began as an improvised theme where the word *crash* aligned with Charlie's playing. It grew to include full chords in the B section that sounded as a fanfare to celebrate Charlie's success. Simple lyric adaptations allow this song to be used with other instruments (*"with the BOOM of the drum"* or the *"RING of the tambourine"*). The song can also be used during a group session to call individuals to play an instrument on cue.

Beat the Drum When You Hear Your Name

Mysterious ♩ = 100

Conio Loretto

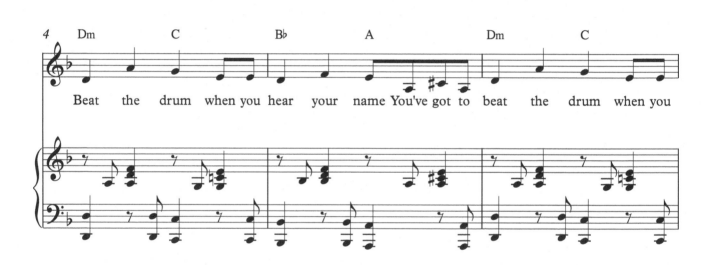

Beat the drum when you hear your name You've got to beat the drum when you

hear your name You've got to beat the drum when you hear your name Your

Raise Your Mallet

Amanda Ruddy Belcastro

Ev' - ry-bo - dy raise your mal-let   Raise your mal-let and crash!

Reach Out

Nicholas Sherman

Reach Up High

Conio Loretto

Copyright © The Center for Discovery, *Songs of Discovery for Music Therapy*, 2023

✱

Three Friends in the Middle

With enthusiasm ♩ = 102

Lee Anne Miller

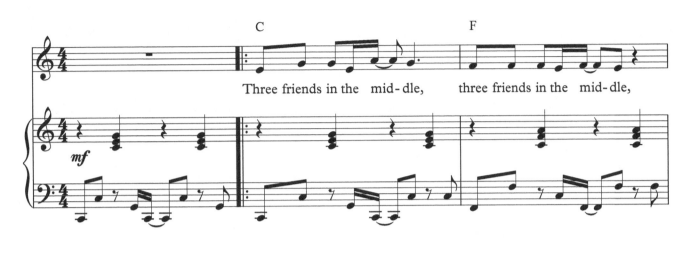

Three friends in the mid-dle,   three friends in the mid-dle,

three friends in the mid-dle to play___   Three friends in the mid-dle,

three friends in the mid-dle,   three friends in the mid-dle to play___

Copyright © The Center for Discovery, *Songs of Discovery for Music Therapy*, 2023

Instruments:
Table Bells
Reed Horn
Tambourine = ♩
Drum = ♩

Up and Down Blues

Amanda Ruddy Belcastro

With the Crash of the Cymbal

Playful ♩ = 118

Conio Loretto

Lyrics: With the crash of the cym-bal we'll make mu-sic With the crash of the cym-bal we'll make mu-sic With the crash of the cym-bal we'll make mu-sic With the crash of the cym-bal we'll make mu-sic And Char-lie can crash Char-lie can

45

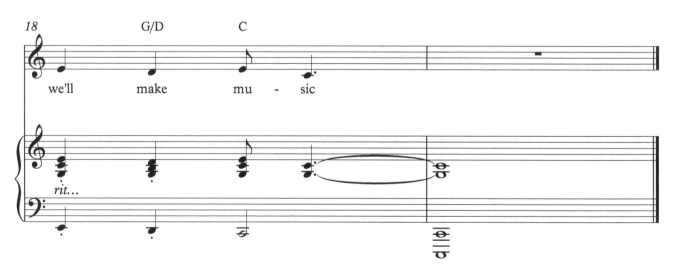

SONGS FOR SELF-AWARENESS AND EMOTIONAL EXPRESSION

I TRIED TO COUNT

Amanda Ruddy Belcastro and Conio Loretto

This song comes from a collection of songs inspired by the children's book *Simon and the Snowflakes* by Giles Tibo.[1] In it, a curious young boy discovers what counts the most as he endeavors to count the impossible. Originally performed by a group of preschoolers for their families and friends, this song became a vehicle for dramatic play in other music therapy sessions. It can also be used as a springboard for children to list what counts the most to them.

I'VE GOT SOMETHING TO SAY

Conio Loretto

Amir came to music therapy with limited capacities for reconciling his deeply felt emotions, which often led to significant behavioral outbursts. Within music therapy, songs composed together with Amir became empowering anthems for his self-expression. The lyrics of "I've Got Something to Say" acknowledge that Amir does, indeed, have something to say and that everyone should take the time to listen to him. During his music therapy sessions, this song often grew into an improvisation that encouraged Amir to verbally express what was on his mind. Other times, the improvisation gave space for Amir to simply vocalize on open sounds and sit with his emotional state.

---

1 Tibo, G. (1988). *Simon and the Snowflakes*. Plattsburgh, NY: Tundra Books.

LET'S SING A SONG ABOUT US

Stacey Hensel

This song was developed over several music therapy sessions with a group of talkative adolescents who were excited to share something meaningful to them. A simple, well-known progression was utilized as a solid musical framework to structure the ideas coming from each group member. In this song, group members are encouraged to come together and sing along in the A section. In the B section, they are encouraged to share something they personally enjoy. The song may be structured such that one idea is shared repeatedly (*"Oh I like to eat pizza – you like to eat pizza"*) or so that one idea may be expanded on (*"Oh I like to eat pizza – you like to eat spaghetti – I like to eat meatballs"*). Additional measures can be added to ensure that each group member has a turn or as a way to restate what everyone previously shared.

SOMETIMES

Amanda Ruddy Belcastro

This song was improvised for a young man who entered the music therapy session room upset and crying. This was an uncharacteristic presentation for him, and he was unable to verbally express the reason for his strong emotions. The opening lyrics and gentle music were improvised to soothe and validate his feelings. In the second half of the song, the music shifts and builds tension with each phrase as the lyrics suggest *"you can cry"* or *"you can scream"* or *"you can yell."* The last lyrical suggestion of *"you don't have to do anything"* came directly from the young man and offered him great comfort and relief. The ending major seventh chords reflect the release in tension as the song concludes in a peaceful, reflective mood.

SOMETIMES YOU JUST HAVE TO WAIT

Conio Loretto

This song was composed for a spirited, strong-willed group of teenagers who all loved being the center of attention. Much of their work in music therapy focused on learning to share the spotlight, work cooperatively, and navigate interpersonal relationships through their co-created music. This playful song was composed to practice waiting for one's turn. The A section explains that *"sometimes you just have to wait,"* with single-note phrases introduced to represent time spent waiting. The B section lists times during the day the group members identified where they might be waiting. In the last section, the group members are finally invited to play the drum, but only after waiting one more time for their names to be announced.

TRAIN ROLLING DOWN THE TRACK

Kenny Farinelli

This song emerged from work with James, a highly excitable young man who was calmly gazing out of the window during one of his music therapy sessions. He spoke the simple phrase *"train rolling down the track,"* which was taken up as lyrics by the therapist who was gently fingerpicking notes on the guitar. The question *"look out the window, what do you see?"* was asked next to invite further responsiveness from James. The song aims to provide a calming, self-guided music and imagery experience. Different sections can be repeated and expanded on to incorporate images suggested by the listener. A pentatonic melody and repetition are used to create a relaxing soundscape.

I Tried to Count

Amanda Ruddy Belcastro
and Conio Loretto

Sweetly ♩ = 94

I tried to count the snow in the sky__ I tried to count the stars and the lights_ But now I know_ what counts the most_ is right there in my

51

✷

I've Got Something to Say

Conio Loretto

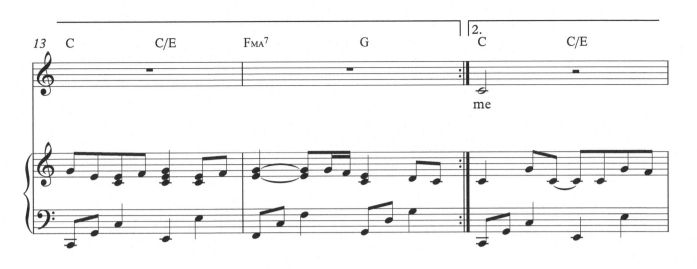

Let's Sing a Song About Us

Stacey Hensel

Sometimes

Peaceful ♪ = 162

Amanda Ruddy Belcastro

Some-times you're sad, some times you're mad Some times you want to

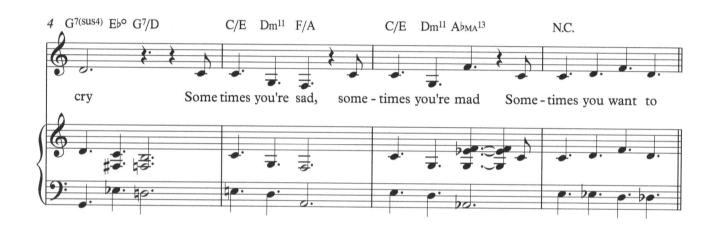

cry Some times you're sad, some - times you're mad Some - times you want to

cry You can cry, you can scream, you can

Sometimes You Just Have to Wait

Gently ♩ = 66

Conio Loretto

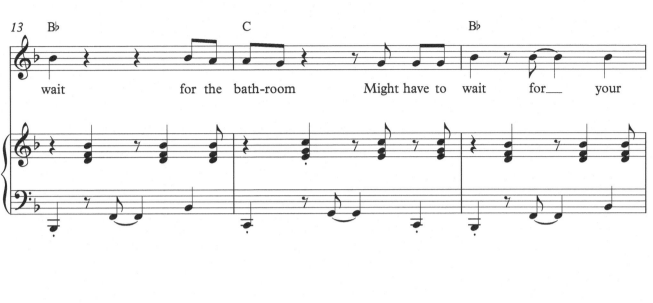

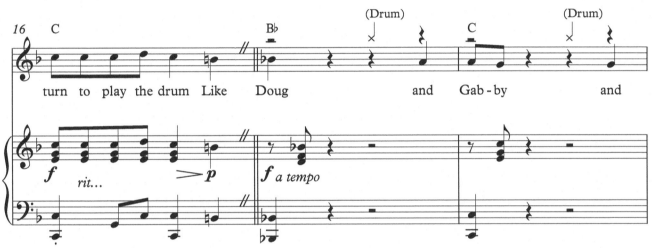

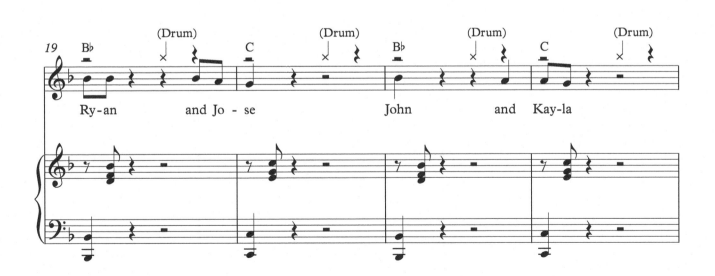

Originally composed
for guitar

Train Rolling Down the Track

Kenny Farinelli

Steady ♩ = 140

We're on a

train rol-ling down the track

Look out the win-dow and what do we see—

Skies so blue and trees so green with you and me

1.

We're on a

SONGS FOR SPECIAL OCCASIONS

TODAY IS YOUR BIRTHDAY

Amanda Ruddy Belcastro, Beth Deyermond, Rebecca Erson, and Conio Loretto

This song was composed for Sophie, a lovely young woman who was celebrating a milestone birthday. Members of the music therapy team who all knew Sophie well collaborated to incorporate elements of Sophie's natural musical responsiveness into a song just for her. For example, highlighted in the song is one of Sophie's frequent melodic and verbal expressions, *"I know,"* often sung with a descending minor third. This, along with the emotional spirit of the music, allowed for a highly personalized, meaningful piece that Sophie could share with those who gathered to celebrate her special day.

HOLIDAY CANDLE COLLECTION

Miyoung Lee and Conio Loretto

* Light the Candles for Hanukkah

* Christmas Candle

* See the Kwanzaa Candles

* Happy New Year

The songs in the Holiday Candle Collection were composed for a group of children to perform at their annual winter showcase. They stand alone as vibrant compositions, each highlighting the role a candle plays in major holidays that fall in December: Hanukkah, Christmas, Kwanzaa, and New Year's Eve. When performed together, however, the candle uniting the songs becomes a symbolic representation of our shared humanity. Beyond performance, the songs have been used within music therapy sessions. Included are optional instrumental parts that can be added when re-creating the songs. Sign language can also be added as another layer of expression.

Today Is Your Birthday

Amanda Ruddy Belcastro, Beth Deyermond,
Rebecca Erson, and Conio Loretto

Light the Candles for Hanukkah

Miyoung Lee and
Conio Loretto

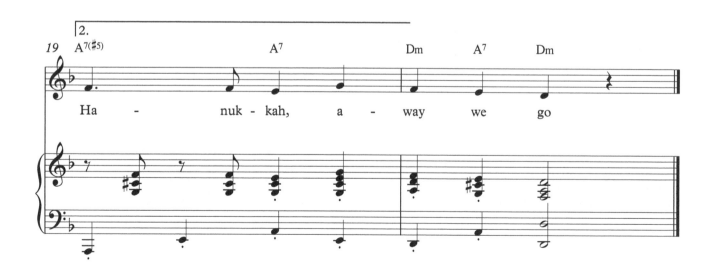

❋

Christmas Candle

Serene ♩ = 72

Miyoung Lee and
Conio Loretto

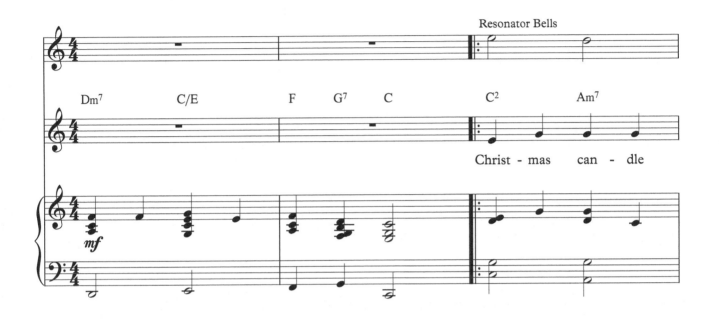

See the Kwanzaa Candles

Miyoung Lee and
Conio Loretto

Happy New Year

Miyoung Lee
and Conio Loretto

RHYTHMIC ADVENTURES

This collection of rhythmic chants comes from a unique initiative developed by a team of music therapists and dance therapists at The Center for Discovery called STOMP, or "Socialization Through Original Music and Movement Programs." STOMP draws on the inherent qualities of rhythm to ground, organize, and connect those engaging in it. Within STOMP sessions, participants are led through a variety of interactive rhythmic exercises, including chants, dances, creative movement, body percussion, drumming, and instrumental play. The overall aim of STOMP is enhanced socialization as participants become engaged in the co-active, shared experiences. Specific outcomes of the program have included improved regulation, focused attention, interactivity, and self-expression.

WELCOME TO STOMP CLASS

Conio Loretto

This lively chant opens every STOMP session. It is important that a solid beat is established and maintained throughout the piece to bring the group members together and focus their energies. Accompaniment can be played on a drum or done with body percussion. Group members are encouraged to open their arms in front of them as they chant the welcoming *"Hello to everyone."* As variation, the lyrics may be adapted to greet one group member at a time (i.e. *"Hello to Grace – Hello to Jackson – Hello to Mason"*). Group members should be encouraged to join in the chant through body percussion before the energized clapping section begins. By putting their whole body into the experience, they can feel a sense of connectedness to the beat, and to each other.

WE GOT THE BEAT

Conio Loretto

Group members join in this chant through the use of body percussion. At the start, group members are encouraged to tap their knees in sync with the established beat. When the lyrics announce *"we've got the beat from our heads to our feet,"* group members should reach up to touch their heads and then down to touch their feet. The lyrics can be adapted to cover other body parts, too, such as, *"we've got the beat from our nose to our toes"* or *"our eyes to our thighs."* During the B section, the leader of the group highlights however group members are expressing the beat (e.g. clapping hands, tapping knees or stomping feet). The lyrics can also shift to name whoever contributes a movement, for example, *"we can clap our hands like Stephen."* Participation in this grounding chant builds self-esteem, creativity, and confidence.

PICKING APPLES FROM THE APPLE TREE

Amanda Ruddy Belcastro, Beth Deyermond, Rebecca Erson, Kenny Farinelli, Conio Loretto, and Nicholas Sherman

WINTER WALK

Amanda Ruddy Belcastro

These high energy, spirited chants were composed to enhance seasonal celebrations. Each contains accompanying movements that are performed alongside the lyrics of the chant, creating fun, dynamic rhythmic experiences.

✻
Welcome to STOMP Class

Rhythmic ♩ = 116

Conio Loretto

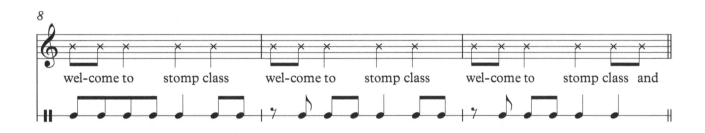

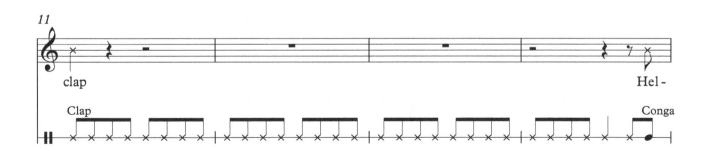

Copyright © The Center for Discovery, *Songs of Discovery for Music Therapy*, 2023

We Got the Beat

Rhythmic ♩ = 116

Conio Loretto

We got the beat, we got the beat, we got the beat, from our head to our feet

Drum

each time rit...

We got the beat, we got the beat, we got the beat, from our head to our feet, from our

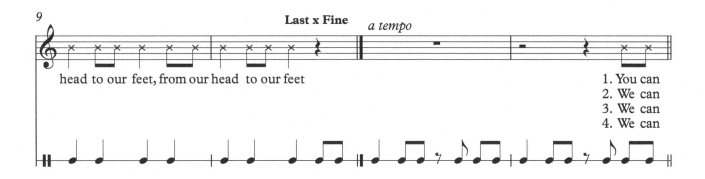

Last x Fine   *a tempo*

head to our feet, from our head to our feet

1. You can
2. We can
3. We can
4. We can

clap your hands,   you can clap your hands,   you can clap your hands,   you can
stomp our feet,   we can stomp our feet,   we can stomp our feet,   we can
pat our knees,   we can pat our knees,   we can pat our knees,   we can
move a - round,   we can move a - round,   we can move a - round,   we can

Picking Apples from the Apple Tree

Amanda Ruddy Belcastro, Beth Deyermond,
Rebecca Erson, Kenny Farinelli,
Conio Loretto, and Nicholas Sherman

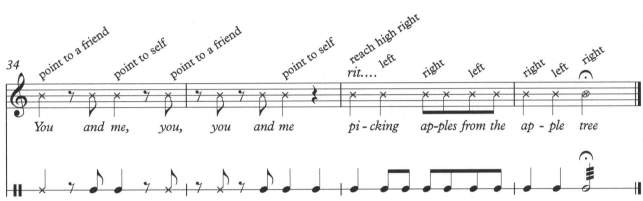

Winter Walk

CLOSING SONGS

ALREADY TIME TO GO

Beth Deyermond

Sometimes it can just be hard to say goodbye. Manny often expressed feelings of disappointment and sadness when it was time for his music therapy session to end, exclaiming *"Oh no!"* which is featured in the lyrics. The added lyrics *"it's already time to go"* recognize that time can seemingly move quickly, but also reinforce that the session is coming to a close. Compositional choices within the song include the use of a descending bassline in the left hand and a consistent eight-note pattern in the right to infuse a sense of sweetness and comfort for the sentiment being expressed.

THANK YOU FOR SHARING

Conio Loretto

This song was composed for Sam, a sensitive young man who often had a difficult time transitioning from one activity to another throughout his school day. When he began in individual music therapy, traditional closing songs made him very anxious and upset as he anticipated the transition out of the session. "Thank you for Sharing" began as an improvisation that expressed gratitude for time spent together in music and celebrated what had been accomplished. These positive affirmations eased the transition into saying *"goodbye,"* which lyrically closes the song and signals that it is time to go. The song is meant to feel like a lullaby—safe, warm, and comforting in its emotional intention.

LOOK AT THAT CLOCK

Kenny Farinelli

This is a buoyant tune originally written for a young man who always checked in on the time during his music therapy sessions. *"What time is it? Are we almost done? How many minutes left?"* Rhythmically, moments of the song are intended to imitate the tick-tock of a clock. Woodblocks or temple blocks can be added during these moments to further illustrate this notion. Additionally, the lyrics can be adapted to center on *hello* rather than *goodbye*. The song itself is useful during times of transition or to prepare for activities that are time dependent.

IT'S TIME TO SAY GOODBYE

Rebecca Erson

The intention of this song is to encourage a settling and winding down of energy at the end of a group music therapy session. The lyrics acknowledge the music that was played and express gratitude for time spent together. The repetitiveness of the lyrics and the soothing feel of the song allow group members to relax and sing along. The song can be easily adapted to vary in tempo or rhythm to meet the energy level expressed by the group members and accommodate their needs in the moment. Extension of the B section allows for a period of reflection as group members listen or play along with the music.

MUSIC IS ALL DONE

Amanda Ruddy Belcastro

This closing song was written for Kathryn, an enthusiastic young woman who communicated through adapted sign language. When signing *"all done"* or *"finished,"* Kathryn would audibly and swiftly swipe her palms together. The motion created a two-beat clap that was the basis for the quick 6/8 feel of the song. Each phrase in the beginning of the song invited Kathryn to joyously complete it with her (clapping) sign. The music then shifts to a more lyrical and legato feeling where Kathryn was inspired to use her voice to sing *"bye."* The song became a staple in Kathryn's music therapy repertoire and ended each session with a playful lightheartedness. It is easily adaptable for other individual or group sessions.

THANK YOU FOR THE MUSIC

Beth Deyermond

Originally an improvised closing song, this became a fixture in Tatyana's music therapy sessions, consistently closing the time spent together each week. The major sevenths in the upper register of the piano provided space that felt light and airy, while the simple bassline comprised of single notes, octaves, and perfect fifths aimed to create a sense of openness and grounding that held Tatyana's bursts of excited energy as the session came to a close.

WE'RE ALL DONE

Amanda Ruddy Belcastro

This song was composed for a group of two teenagers who anxiously anticipated the ending of their sessions. The slow, gospel-like progression provided a soothing foundation that prepared both for the transition out of the session. The familiar phrase *"we're all done"* seemed to comfort the pair, who would participate by using adapted sign language when cued by the music. In the second half of the song, the contrary motion of the bassline and melody continues the calming mood while the repetition of the word *"goodbye"* encourages singing along towards the final measure of the piece.

Already Time to Go

With emotion ♩ = 78

Beth Deyermond

Oh no, oh no, it's al-rea-dy time to go_ It's time to say good-bye time to

say good- bye Oh no, oh no, it's al-rea-dy time to go_ it's time to say good-bye for

now Time to___ say___ good-bye Sor-ry, but it's time to

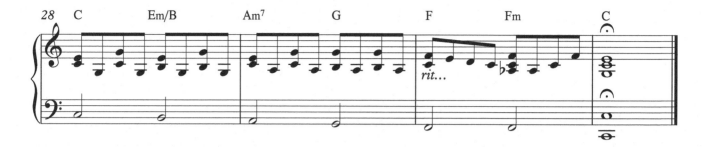

Thank You for Sharing

Conio Loretto

now it's time to say_____ good - bye_____

✳

Look at that Clock

Kenny Farinelli

It's Time to Say Goodbye

Rebecca Erson

*

Music Is All Done

Quick ♪ = 200

Amanda Ruddy Belcastro

Thank You for the Music

With emotion ♩ = 78

Beth Deyermond

We're All Done

Sweetly ♩ = 74

Amanda Ruddy Belcastro

Lyrics:
We're all done. We're all done. We're all done. Good-bye, good-bye. Good-bye, good-bye. Good bye, good-bye, good-bye.

GOAL IMPLICATIONS BY SONG

	Emotional awareness	Group cohesion	Improvising expressively	Joint attention	Language building	Motor skills	Name recognition	Number concepts	Peer interactions	Playing on cue	Taking turns	Verbal – vocal expression
Beat the Drum to Say Hello				★		★				★	★	
Welcome Back		★										★
Welcome Back to the Music Room		★					★				★	★
Beat the Drum When You Hear Your Name				★		★	★			★	★	
Raise Your Mallet		★		★		★			★	★	★	
Reach Up High			★			★						
Three Friends in the Middle		★	★	★				★	★			
Up and Down Blues		★				★			★	★	★	
With a Crash of the Cymbal			★			★	★			★		
Reach Out			★			★	★					
I Tried to Count	★				★			★				★

	Emotional awareness	Group cohesion	Improvising expressively	Joint attention	Language building	Motor skills	Name recognition	Number concepts	Peer interactions	Playing on cue	Taking turns	Verbal – vocal expression
I've Got Something to Say	★				★							★
Let's Sing a Song About Us	★	★			★		★				★	★
Sometimes	★				★							★
Sometimes You Just Have to Wait	★	★		★	★	★	★			★	★	
Train Rolling Down the Track	★				★							★
Today Is Your Birthday					★		★					★
Light the Candles for Hanukkah		★		★	★	★			★	★		★
Christmas Candle		★		★	★	★				★	★	★
See the Kwanzaa Candles		★		★	★	★			★	★	★	
Happy New Year					★							★
Welcome to STOMP Class		★	★	★	★	★	★		★			★
We Got the Beat		★	★	★	★	★	★		★		★	
Picking Apples from the Apple Tree/ Winter Walk		★		★	★	★						★
Already Time to Go	★				★							★
Thank You for Sharing					★							★

	Emotional awareness	Group cohesion	Improvising expressively	Joint attention	Language building	Motor skills	Name recognition	Number concepts	Peer interactions	Playing on cue	Taking turns	Verbal – vocal expression
Look at that Clock					★		★					★
It's Time to Say Goodbye					★							★
Music Is All Done					★	★						★
Thank You for the Music					★							★
We're All Done					★	★						★